ONE HUNDRED WAYS
TO

Comfort

ONE HUNDRED WAYS
TO

Comfort

COMPILED BY

Celia Haddon

Hodder & Stoughton
LONDON SYDNEY AUCKLAND

British Library Cataloguing in Publication Data
A record for this book is available from
the British Library

ISBN 0 340 74602 5

Printed and bound in Great Britain
by Clays Ltd, St Ives plc

Hodder and Stoughton
A division of Hodder Headline Ltd
338 Euston Road
London NW1 3BH

Contents

Loss and Bereavement

Love is not changed by Death,
And nothing is lost and all in the end is
harvest.

EDITH SITWELL,
poet, 1887–1964

If the dead, and we, be not upon one floor, nor under one storey, yet we are under one roof. We think not a friend lost, because he is gone into another room, nor because he is gone into another land; and into another world, no man is gone, for that heaven, which God created, and this world, is all one world.

JOHN DONNE,
poet and clergyman, 1572–1631

He was my North, my South, my East
   and West,
My working week and my Sunday rest,
My noon, my midnight, my talk, my
   song;
I thought that love would last for ever:
   I was wrong.

The stars are not wanted now; put out
   every one:
Pack up the moon and dismantle the
   sun;
Pour away the ocean and sweep up
   the woods:
For nothing now can ever come to any
   good.

W.H. AUDEN,
poet, 1907–73

The death of friends should inspire us as much as their lives.

Henry David Thoreau, philosopher, 1817–62

Death is nothing at all. It does not count ... Call me by the old familiar name. Speak of me in the easy way which you always used. Put no difference into your tone. Wear no forced air of solemnity or sorrow. Laugh as we always laughed at the little jokes that we enjoyed together. Play, smile, think of me, pray for me. Let my name be ever the household word that it always was ... I am waiting for you, for an interval, somewhere very near, just round the corner. All is well. Nothing is hurt; nothing is lost ...

HENRY SCOTT HOLLAND,
clergyman, 1847–1918

Remember – won't you? – that [the pain] is a sign of the success of your relationship with each other … Inevitably there will be things which you will wish had been different. There always are – and I

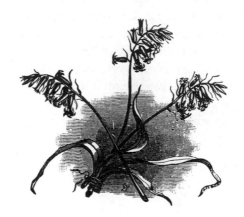

suppose always will be until humanity
becomes perfect. This constant under-
ground worry of 'if only I'd done ...'
whatever it may be, is an inevitable
part of dying for those of us who
have tried to help. Perhaps what
matters is that we can hang on to
understanding. The one thing which
any genuine love brings is surely
that, and I sometimes think it is un-
fair to the people we have loved and
still do, if we assume for them that
they would not understand why we
did whatever it was.

MARGARET J. CHALLIS,
headmistress, 1917–94

Our friends leave us for a while –
they do but go before; they are
not destroyed by death – they enter
into Eternity.

ST AMBROSE,
bishop, 339–97

When I must leave you for a little while,
Please do not grieve and shed wild
    tears
And hug your sorrow to you through
    the years.
But start out bravely with a gallant
    smile;
And for my sake and in my name
Live on and do all things the same.
Feed not your loneliness on empty
    days,
But fill each waking hour in useful
    ways,
Reach out your hand in comfort and in
    cheer
And I in turn will comfort you and
    hold you near.

AUTHOR UNKNOWN

There is nothing, no, nothing innocent or good, that dies, and is forgotten. Let us hold to that faith, or none. An infant, a prattling child, dying in its cradle, will live again in the better thoughts of those who loved it; and play its part, through them, in the redeeming actions of the world, though its body be burned to ashes or drowned in the deepest sea.

CHARLES DICKENS,
novelist, 1812–70

Even for the dead I will not bind my
 soul to grief;
Death cannot long divide.
Is it not as though the rose that
 climbed my garden wall had
 blossomed on the other side?
Death doth but hide but not divide.

AUTHOR UNKNOWN

Death is only an horizon and an horizon is nothing save the limit of our sight.

Attrib. FR BEDE JARRETT,
Dominican friar, 1881–1934

I believe those who truly love are already twined together in a world far beyond and behind the visible – and in that world they are safe – and their love is safe – from the storms of time and misadventure.

EDWARD CARPENTER,
poet and social reformer, 1844–1929

If we still love those we lose, can we altogether lose those we love?

AUTHOR UNKNOWN

All whom we loved, and all who loved us, whom we still love no less, while they love us yet more, are ever near, because ever in his presence in whom we live and dwell.

HENRY EDWARD MANNING,
cardinal, 1808–92

In the quietness of this place I think of her with the love and understanding that still join us together. I remember her goodness and the blessings I received through her. Her memory is precious to me and is always with me.

May her memory continue to strengthen me and guide me. Because life is short, let me fill it with acts of goodness, let me be broader in my sympathies, and purer in my motives. Help me to learn the meaning and value of life. Help me to know that goodness is not in vain, and the grave is not the end.

PRAYERS ON VISITING A GRAVE
from the Funeral Service of the
Reform Synagogues of
Great Britain

Trouble or Despair

He said not: 'Thou shalt not be tempested, thou shalt not be travailed, thou shalt not be afflicted.' But he said, 'Thou shalt not be overcome.'

DAME JULIAN OF NORWICH, anchoress, *c.*1343–after 1442

Be pleased to remember that there are bright stars under the most palpable clouds, and light is never so beautiful as in the presence of darkness.

HENRY VAUGHAN,
poet, 1622–95

The person who doesn't make mistakes, doesn't make anything.

AUTHOR UNKNOWN

When some great sorrow like a
    mighty river
Flows through your life with peace-
    destroying power,
And the dearest things are swept
    from sight for ever,
Say to yourself each trying hour,
'This too will pass away.'

AUTHOR UNKNOWN

If a thousand plans fail, be not disheartened. As long as your purposes are right, you have not failed.

THOMAS DAVIDSON,
poet and preacher, 1838–70

Dear God, be good to me; the sea is so wide, and my boat is so small.

A BRETON FISHERMAN'S PRAYER

You will come out from your grief stronger than when you entered it.

ALEXANDRE DUMAS,
novelist, 1802–70

OLord, remember not only the men and women of good will, but also those of ill will. But do not remember all the suffering they have inflicted on us; remember the fruits we have bought thanks to this suffering – our comradeship, our loyalty, our humility, our courage, our generosity, the greatness of heart which has grown out of all this, and when they come to judgment let all the fruits which we have borne be their forgiveness.

UNKNOWN PRISONER
in Ravensbruck concentration camp

Our greatest glory is, not in never falling, but in rising every time we fall.

OLIVER GOLDSMITH,
writer, 1728–74

Often we shall have to change the direction of our thinking and our wishing and our striving. That is what repentance really means – taking our bearings afresh and trying a new road.

HARRY WILLIAMS,
living clergyman

There are two great pillars that bear us up, amid the wreck of misfortune and misery. The one is composed of the different modifications of a certain noble, stubborn something in man, known by the names of courage, fortitude, magnanimity. The other is made up of ... those senses of the mind ... which connect us with, and link us to, those obscure realities – an all-powerful God, and a world to come, beyond death and the grave.

ROBERT BURNS,
poet, 1759–96

Despair lames most people, but it wakes others fully up.

WILLIAM JAMES,
psychologist and philosopher,
1842–1910

It is perhaps better to make the mistakes of facing life than to make the mistakes of running away from life.

HAVELOCK ELLIS,
sex researcher and writer,
1859–1939

Living Through the Pain

Endurance ... is the last offering, the highest act of the child of God ... Sometimes everything goes but the power of enduring.

GEORGE HOWARD WILKINSON,
bishop, 1833–1907

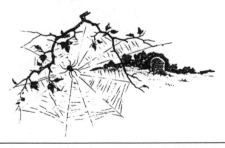

Keep on
keeping on.

Attrib. WILLIAM BOOTH,
Salvation Army founder,
1829–1912

I believe that the wisest plan of bearing sorrow is sometimes not to try to bear it – as long as one is not crippled for one's everyday duties – but to give way to sorrow, utterly and freely. Perhaps sorrow is sent that we MAY give way to it, and, in drinking the cup to the dregs, find some medicine in it itself which we should not find if we began doctoring ourselves, or letting others doctor us.

CHARLES KINGSLEY,
writer, 1819–75

How can I live my lonesome days?
How can I tread my lonesome ways?
How can I take my lonesome meal?
Or how outlive the grief I feel?

WILLIAM BARNES,
poet, 1800–86

Be like the promontory against which the waves continually break, but it stands firm and tames the fury of the water around it.

MARCUS AURELIUS,
Roman emperor and philosopher,
121–180

To bear is to conquer our fate.

THOMAS CAMPBELL,
poet, 1777–1844

I do abhor sentimentality from the bottom of my soul, and cannot wear my grief upon my sleeve, but yet I look forward with agony to the time when she may become a memory instead of a constant presence.

JAMES RUSSELL LOWELL,
poet, 1819–91

The only way out of emotional pain is through it.

AUTHOR UNKNOWN

The law of worthy life is funda-mentally the law of strife. It is only through labour and painful effort, by grim energy and resolute courage, that we move on to better things.

THEODORE ROOSEVELT,
American president, 1858–1919

Pain has an element of blank;
It cannot recollect
When it began, or if there were
A day when it was not.

It has no future but itself,
Its infite realms contain
Its past, enlightened to perceive
New periods of pain.

EMILY DICKINSON,
poet, 1830–86

To endure all things with a steady and peaceful mind not only brings with it many blessings to the soul, but also enables us, in the midst of our difficulties, to have a clear judgment about them, and to supply the fitting remedy for them.

ST JOHN OF THE CROSS,
mystic, 1542–91

G od does not give us more than
we can endure – though he cuts
it pretty fine at times.

AUTHOR UNKNOWN

L ook upon each day that comes as
a challenge, as a test of courage.
The pain will come in waves, some
days worse than others, for no
apparent reason. Accept the pain.
Do not suppress it. Never attempt to
hide grief from yourself.

DAPHNE DU MAURIER,
writer, 1907–89

Yea, though I walk through the valley of the shadow of death, I will fear no evil: for thou art with me; thy rod and thy staff they comfort me.

PSALM 23

Never mind the ridicule, never mind the defeat: up again, old heart!

RALPH WALDO EMERSON,
essayist, 1803–82

O heart, hold thee secure
In this blind hour of stress,
Live on, love on, endure,
Uncowed, though comfortless.

WALTER DE LA MARE,
poet, 1873–1956

Help us with the grace of courage that we be none of us cast down when we sit lamenting amid the ruins of our happiness or our integrity: touch us with fire from the altar, that we may be up and doing to rebuild our city.

ROBERT LOUIS STEVENSON,
writer, 1850–94

When it hurts, it's healing.

DANNY BRESLIN,
railway worker, died 1989

Ways of Coping

A period in the wilderness, if it serves no other purpose, does at least help one to get one's priorities in order. The things once assumed to be essential for one's life, such as the constant company of other people, society's approval, one's own reput-ation amongt those who amount to something in the world's eyes, and the number of important people one knows seem suddenly to dissolve like a mist of unreality.

MARTIN ISRAEL,
living clergyman and writer

For there is ... no man that imparteth his griefs to his friend, but he grieveth the less.

SIR FRANCIS BACON,
philosopher, 1561–1626

There remain times when one can only endure. One lives on, one does not die, and the only thing that one can do is to fill one's mind and time as far as possible with the concerns of other people. It doesn't bring immediate peace, but it brings the dawn nearer.

ARTHUR CHRISTOPHER BENSON,
writer, 1862–1925

Trouble and perplexity drive us to prayer, and prayer driveth away trouble and perplexity.

PHILIP MELANCHTHON,
theologian and reformer, 1497–1560

Give sorrow words. The grief that
    does not speak
Whispers the o'er-fraught heart, and
    bids it break.

WILLIAM SHAKESPEARE,
playwright, 1564–1616

It is right to weep and mourn …
The tears release the tension;
Take courage – remember happy
   days
You shared – and though you are
   sad,
Carry on as they would have you,
Living, loving, laughing, caring …

AUTHOR UNKNOWN

If you find yourself, as I dare say you sometimes do, overpowered as it were by melancholy, the best way is to go out and do something kind to somebody or other. Writing, too, I have known in many cases a very great relief … I fancy the best way would be to write on till one was a little unburthened, and then put one's confessions in the fire.

JOHN KEBLE,
poet and clergyman, 1792–1866

The best thing for being sad is to learn something. That is the only thing that never fails ... That is the only thing which the mind can never exhaust, never alienate, never be tortured by, never fear or distrust, and never dream of regretting.

T.H. WHITE,
novelist, 1906–64

There are few things more con-
soling to men than the mere
finding that other men have felt as
they feel.

FREDERICK W. FABER,
theologian, 1814–63

For my part, when I am tempted to doubt the goodness of God, and the essential sanity of the universe, the first challenge that I have to meet is the challenge of Beauty – the sheer beauty of God's world.

GEOFFREY STUDDERT KENNEDY,
clergyman, 1883–1929

O dreamy, gloomy, friendly trees,
I came along your narrow track
To bring my gifts unto your knees
And gifts did you bring back:
For when I brought this heart that
    burns –
These thoughts that bitterly repine –
And laid them here among the ferns,
And the hum of boughs divine,
Ye vastest breathers of the air,
Shook down with slow and mighty
    poise
Your coolness on the human care,
Your wonder on its toys,
Your greenness on the heart's despair,
Your darkness on its noise.

HERBERT TRENCH,
poet, 1865–1923

During a period of deep public unhappiness when at times it seemed that all I had striven for lay in ruins around me, I listed off those things that brought the blessed counterpoint of happiness. I wrote: 'Privately I have been blessed with abundant happiness with Julia and our life together, the most precious and miraculous gift of all. Our house, my writing room, the garden and its changing seasons, give me perpetual joy.'

SIR ROY STRONG,
living historian, writer and gardener

Bethink thee of something that thou oughtest to do, and go and do it, if it be but the sweeping of a room, or the preparing of a meal, or a visit to a friend; heed not thy feelings: do thy work.

GEORGE MACDONALD,
writer, 1824–1905

Make yourself nests of pleasant thoughts ... Bright fancies, satisfied memories, noble histories, faithful sayings, treasure houses of precious and restful thoughts, which care cannot disturb, nor pain make gloomy, nor poverty take away from us – houses built without hands, for our souls to live in.

JOHN RUSKIN,
critic, 1819–1900

Finding a Meaning

Let me suggest that the bad things that happen to us in our lives do not have a meaning when they happen to us. They do not happen for any good reason which would cause us to accept them willingly. But we can give them a meaning. We can redeem these tragedies from sense-lessness by imposing meaning on them.

HAROLD KUSHNER,
living rabbi

A man may fulfil the object of his existence by asking a question he cannot answer, and attempting a task he cannot achieve.

OLIVER WENDELL HOLMES,
writer and doctor, 1809–94

To those who have large capability of loving and suffering, united with great power of firm endurance, there comes a time in their woe when they are lifted out of the contemplation of their individual case into the searching inquiry into the nature of their calamity, and the remedy (if remedy there be) which may prevent its recurrence to others as well as to themselves.

ELIZABETH GASKELL,
novelist, 1810–65

God has created me to do him some definite service. He has committed some work to me which he has not committed to another. I have my mission. I may never know it in this life, but I shall be told it in the next. I am a link in a chain, a bond of connection between persons. He has not created me for naught. I shall do good. I shall do his work. I shall be an angel of peace, a preacher of truth in my own place while not intending it – if I do but keep his commandments.

Therefore I will trust him. Whatever, wherever I am. I can never be thrown away. If I am in sickness, my sickness may serve him; in perplexity, my perplexity may serve him; if I am

in sorrow, my sorrow may serve him.
He does nothing in vain. He knows
what he is about.

JOHN HENRY NEWMAN,
cardinal, 1801–90

Life has meaning only in the struggle. Triumph and defeat are in the hands of the gods. So let us celebrate the struggle.

SWAHILI SONG

The way in which a man accepts his fate and all the suffering it entails, the way in which he takes up his cross, gives him ample opportunity – even under the most difficult circumstances – to add a deeper meaning to his life. It may remain brave, dignified, and unselfish.

VICTOR FRANKL,
psychiatrist and concentration camp
survivor, 1905–97

To shirk pain, bearable pain, altogether is not only to be less real than one might have been: it is to isolate oneself from the common lot of pain, from the pain of humanity and the world. It is to blunt or cut off or withdraw one's antennae; it is to play only such notes as one chooses in the universal symphony, which is a symphony of suffering as well as joy.

VICTOR GOLLANCZ,
publisher, 1893–1967

Oh yet we trust that somehow good
Will be the final goal of ill,
To pangs of nature, wins of will,
Defects of doubt, and taints of
  blood.

That nothing walks with aimless feet;
That not one life shall be destroyed,
Or cast as rubbish to the void,
When God hath made the pile
  complete.

ALFRED TENNYSON,
poet, 1809–92

I believe in the sun, even when it is not shining. I believe in love, even when I do not feel it. I believe in God, even when he is silent.

LINES ON A CELLAR WALL IN COLOGNE,
after its destruction
by bombing, 1944

Take courage, and turn your troubles, which are without remedy, into material for spiritual progress.

FRANCIS DE SALES,
bishop, writer and novelist, 1567–1622

It is certain that we never think or strive to solve a problem unless it hurts us to leave it unsolved, and many of us will not move unless an unsolved problem hurts us very badly. We need a pain, and a very sharp pain, before we are willing to face the effort of thought.

GEOFFREY STUDDERT KENNEDY,
clergyman, 1883–1929

The compensations of calamity are made apparent to the understanding also, after long intervals of time. A fever, a mutilation, a cruel disappointment, a loss of wealth, a loss of friends, seems at the moment unpaid loss, and unpayable. But the sure years reveal the deep remedial force that underlies all facts.

RALPH WALDO EMERSON,
essayist, 1803–82

Acceptance

Nothing is ever really lost, or can be lost,
No birth, identity, form – no object of
   the world,
Nor life, nor force, nor any visible thing;
Appearance must not foil, nor shifted
   sphere confuse thy brain ...
The light in the eye grown dim, shall
   duly flame again;
The sun now low in the west rises for
   morning and for noons continual;
To frozen clods ever the spring's invisible
   law returns,
With grass and flowers and summer
   fruits and corn.

WALT WHITMAN,
poet, 1819–91

For the first sharp pangs there is no comfort ... But slowly, the clinging companionship with the dead is linked with our living affections and duties, and we begin to feel our sorrow as a solemn initiation, preparing us for that sense of loving, pitying fellowship with the fullest human lot which, I must think, no one who has tasted it will deny to be the chief blessedness of our life.

GEORGE ELIOT,
novelist, 1819–80

If, as I can't help suspecting, the dead also feel the pains of separation (and this may be one of their purgatorial sufferings), then for both lovers, and for all pairs of lovers without exception, bereavement is a universal and integral part of our experience of love. It follows marriage as normally as marriage follows courtship or as autumn follows summer ... What we want is to live our marriage well and faithfully through that phase too. If it hurts (and it certainly will) we accept the pains as a necessary part of this phase.

C.S. LEWIS,
scholar and writer, 1898–1963

The dead are gone and with them
   we cannot converse.
The living are here and ought to
   have our love.
Leaving the city-gate I look ahead
And see before me only mounds and
   tombs …
I want to go home, to ride to my
   village gate.
I want to go back, but there's no
   road back.

Translated from the Chinese by
ARTHUR WALEY,
oriental scholar, 1889–1966

The vision of glory must always outweigh the suffering and hells of evil that have happened in my life's spell. And still happen. We may lose sight of the glory over and over again, but that does not mean that the glory is not there.

ANNE SHELLS,
living painter

We must press on, whether we will or no, and we shall walk better with our eyes before us than with them ever cast behind.

JEROME K. JEROME,
writer, 1857–1927

Our whole trouble in our lot in this world rises from the disagreement of our mind therewith. Let the mind be brought to the lot, and the whole tumult is instantly hushed; let it be kept in that disposition, and the man shall stand at ease, in his affliction, like a rock unmoved with waters beating upon it.

THOMAS BOSTON,
theologian, 1677–1732

When I am dead, cry for me a little.
Think of me sometimes, but not too
　much.
Think of me now and again as I was
　in life
At some moment that is pleasant to
　recall,
But not for long.
Leave me in peace, and I shall leave
　you in peace.
And while you live,
Let your thoughts be with the living.

A NATIVE AMERICAN PRAYER

Eventually instead of memories being an intense form of torture, they gradually cease to wound, and some of them even become quietly pleasing and warm. Eventually, too, in a remarkable way the dead person seems to have become part of yourself. Some of their opinions, skills, insight and values are intermingled with your own, and in this way they have left the strongest legacy.

AGNES WHITAKER,
writer, 1935–86

The past exists only in memory, consequences and effect. It has power over me only as I give it my power. I can let go, release it, move on freely. I am not the past.

AUTHOR UNKNOWN

Ah, if you knew what peace there is in accepted sorrow.

JEANNE GUYON,
mystic, 1648–1717

I have indeed fought through a hell of terrors and horrors (which none could know but myself) in a divided existence; now no longer divided nor at war with myself, I shall travel on in the strength of the Lord God.

WILLIAM BLAKE,
poet and mystic, 1757–1827

We learn wisdom from failure much more than from success. We often discover what will do, by finding out what will not do.

SAMUEL SMILES,
social reformer, 1812–1904

There is no separation – no past; eternity, the Now, is continuous. When all the stars have revolved they only produce Now again. The continuity of Now is for ever.

RICHARD JEFFERIES,
writer, 1848–87

The innocent brightness of a new
    born day
Is lovely yet.

WILLIAM WORDSWORTH,
poet, 1770–1850

The Spiritual Journey

Every man has two journeys to make through life. There is the outer journey, with its various incidents and the milestones … There is also an inner journey, a spiritual odyssey, with a secret history of its own.

WILLIAM R. INGE,
dean, 1860–1954

Earth's crammed with heaven,
And every common bush afire with
  God.

ELIZABETH BARRET BROWNING,
poet, 1806–61

It is in the silence that follows the storm, not in the silence that comes before it, that we should look for the budding of the flower.

HINDU SAYING

If you hate God, then for Christ's sake tell him you do and tell him why. By having the courage of your aggression you will show greater trust in him and greater love for him than by all that 'resigned submissive meek' stuff which leaves you to take the hell out of other people, and not least out of yourself.

HARRY A. WILLIAMS,
living clergyman

My son, I am the Lord, that giveth strength in the day of tribulation … Trust in me and put thy confidence in my mercy. When thou thinkest thyself farthest off from me, oftentimes I am nearest unto thee.

ST THOMAS À KEMPIS,
monk, 1379–1471

Even when the gates of heaven are closed to prayer, they are open to tears.

THE TALMUD

At the close of life, the question is –
Not how much you have got,
But how much you have given.
Not how much you have won,
But how much you have done.
Not how much you have saved,
But how much you have sacrificed.
Not how much you were honoured,
But how much you have loved and
    served.

AUTHOR UNKNOWN

Nor can we fall below the arms of God, how low soever it be we fall.

WILLIAM PENN,
Quaker, 1644–1718

Console yourself, you would not seek me, if you had not found me.

BLAISE PASCAL,
mathematician and theologian,
1623–62

For thou lovest all the things that are, and abhorrest nothing which thou has made; for never wouldst thou have made anything, if thou hadst hated it. And how could anything have endured, if it had not been thy will? Or been preserved, if not called by thee? But thou sparest all; for they are thine, O Lord, thou lover of souls.

THE WISDOM OF SOLOMON,
THE APROCRYPHA

Dear Lord,
Help me to live this day
Quietly, easily;
To lean upon thy great strength,
Trustfully, restfully;
To wait for the unfolding of thy will
Patiently, serenely,
To meet others
Peacefully, joyously;
To face tomorrow
Confidently, courageously.

Attrib. St Francis of Assisi,
friar, 1182–1226

When thou passest through the waters, I will be with thee; and through the rivers, they shall not overflow thee: when thou walkest through the fire, thou shalt not be burned; neither shall the flame kindle upon thee …

Fear not, for I am with thee.

ISAIAH, OLD TESTAMENT

Are not five sparrows sold for two farthings, and not one of them is forgotten before God? But even the very hairs of your head are all numbered. Fear not therefore: you are of more value than many sparrows.

JESUS CHRIST

Acknowledgments

There are some copyrights in this book which I could not trace. The publishers will be happy to rectify any omissions in future editions. I would like to thank the following for permission to reprint:

Beacon Press for an extract from *Man's Search for Meaning* by Viktor E. Frankl, copyright © 1959, 1962, 1984, 1992 by Viktor E. Frankl. Reprinted by permission of Beacon Press, Boston.

Cassell & Co for an extract from *More for Timothy* by Victor Gollancz, published by Victor Gollancz, Cassell & Co.

The estate of Margaret J. Challis for an extract from an unpublished letter written to Celia Haddon.

Constable & Robinson Ltd for an extract from *The True Wilderness* by Harry A. Williams, published by Constable Publishers Ltd.

Curtis Brown for an extract from the *Rebecca Notebook & Other Memories* by Daphne du Maurier. Reproduced with permission of Curtis Brown Ltd, London, on behalf of the Chichester Partnership. Copyright © 1981 by Daphne du Maurier.

Darton Longman and Todd for an extract from *All in the End is Harvest*, edited by Agnes Whitaker, published and copyright © 1984 by Darton Longman and Todd in association with Cruse

Bereavement Care, and used by the permission of the publishers.

English Province of the Order of Preachers, St Dominic's Priory, for permission to quote an extract from a prayer by Bede Jarrett.

Faber and Faber Ltd for two verses from 'Twelve Songs IX' ("Stop all the clocks...") by W.H. Auden, taken from *Collected Poems* by W.H. Auden and published by Faber and Faber Ltd, and for an extract from *A Grief Observed* by C.S. Lewis, published by Faber and Faber Ltd.

HarperCollins for an extract from *Tensions* by Harry A. Williams.

Harvard University Press for 'Pain has an element of blank', reprinted by perrmission of the publishers and the Trustees of Amherst College from *The Poems of Emily Dickinson*, edied by Ralph W. Franklin, published by the Belknap Press of Harvard University Press, and copyright © 1951, 1955, 1979, 1998 by the President and Fellows of Harvard College.

David Higham Associates for two lines from 'Euridice' by Edith Sitwell, taken from *Collected Poems* by Edith Sitwell and published by Sinclair Stevenson, and for an extract from *The Sword in the Stone* by T.H. White, published by HarperCollins.

Hodder and Stoughton for an extract from *Man's Search for Meaning* by Victor Frankl. Reproduced by permission of Hodder and Stoughton Limited.

Professor François Lafitte for a passage by Havelock Ellis.